All Manner of

Prayer

The Heart of an Intercessor

Alice J. Jones

Purpose Publishing
1503 Main Street #168 ♨ Grandview, Missouri
www.purposepublishing.com

ISBN: 978-0692557303

Editing by TWA Media Team
Book Cover Design by LPW Designs LLC

The Scripture verses and passages in this book were not taken from any one version or translation of the Bible. Unless otherwise noted, combined portions of various translations were used to more accurately portray or expand on the intended meaning.

Printed in the United States of America

Dedication

Prayer was something I observed as a small child in the life of my natural father, which created a desire to learn and grow. But most of all I give thanks to my heavenly father who taught me through every circumstance that I ought always pray.

To my wonderful husband Bishop DK jones, who maintains a continual position of intercession before the throne of grace on my behalf.

Thanks to my spiritual mother Sylvia Mom "T" Turner, whose life of prayer has challenged, encouraged, and tirelessly covered my life, family and ministry.

Thanks to the mighty prayer warriors of TWA of Indianapolis, who have been like disciples allowing me to teach them to pray.

And to all those who inspired and caused me to pray

-Thank you

Book Reviews

"All Manner Of Prayer"...This book is a must read, and I encourage you to consistently listen to these prayers through Apostle Alice J. Jones! As a pastor and overseer of ministries, I have personally shared and endorsed ALL MANNER OF PRAYER as a teaching tool fashioned to set the captive free from bondage on three dimensions: spirit, soul and body

Bishop Virgil Patterson, Crusade Christian Faith Center
Los Angeles, California

After reading the first line of "All Manner of Prayer" I knew I was in for a life altering experience. Being a woman of prayer, this tool of prayer allowed me to engage in effectual fervent communication with my Heavenly Father. Apostle Jones clearly defines prayer and shares, most of all, that prayer is our devoted fellowship with our Father and teaches that daily prayer in the life of a believer is as vital as the air we breathe. If you want a deeper relationship with God through prayer, I encourage you to saturate yourself in the Word of God through All Manner of Prayer"!

Teresa Sims

Through the years Apostle Jones' ministry has blessed me. I play the "All Manner of Prayer "cd over and over again. I personally can attest to its impact after experiencing a divine financial increase of $14,000.00 while believing God's word and praying "Breakthrough Prayer." I recommend you get this powerful kingdom resource in your possession today.

Pastor Lorraine,

Crusade Christian Faith Center
Los Angeles, California

"All Manner of Prayer is an excellent way to transition into the very presence of God. It places all of the focus on Him and His word while fulfilling the truth of Romans 10:17 that faith come by hearing and hearing by the word of God. I have been extremely blessed by it and would definitely recommend it for others who desire meaningful fellowship with the Lord in prayer."

Bro. Aaron Hopson

Gems from Joy Ministries
Southfield, MI

Table of Prayers

Introduction

The power and the privilege of all true believers is to communicate with our heavenly Father through prayer.

Prayer can be expressed in praise, supplication, by petition, declaration, worship, in a tear, a shout, a quiet moment in His presence, a song, a groan, or even a faith confession.

Prayer to the believer is as necessary as the air we breathe. When we grow faint and weary through the trials of this world, we must remember the words that Jesus taught. Jesus said, "Men ought always to pray and not faint." (Luke 18:1 AMP)

In this hour, prayer is the much needed and vital spiritual discipline that will sustain, strengthen, and keep us in our day-to-day lives. Ephesians 6:18 exhorts us to "Pray at all times (on every occasion, in every season) in the Spirit, with all [manner of] prayer and entreaty. To that end, keep alert and watch with strong purpose and perseverance, interceding on behalf of all the saints (God's consecrated *er's* dictionary defines "manner" as a a way of doing something.

Prayer is a wonderful aid toward becoming prayer. It provides insightful directives and personal prayer petitions from the word of God. Through many seasons of my life, I have found strength, direction, energy, comfort, forgiveness, and grace to continue as I experienced the many facets of prayer.

My desire is to share these written expressions of prayer with every believer who will take God at His Word and pray with *All Manner of Prayer.*

Morning Prayer

Psalm 118:24

"This is the day which the LORD hath made; we will rejoice and be glad in it."

There is a river whose streams make glad the city of our God! Lord you are the river of life, your spirit flows within me, therefore I will rejoice in you always, and again I will rejoice. Yes you Father are in the midst of me, and you rejoice over me and will help me throughout this day. I will not be moved by any adverse circumstances, no matter what comes.

I awake the dawn with singing and rejoicing, for my hope is in you! I rise and shine and am radiant, for your glory is upon me. I put on the garment of praise and silence every enemy arrayed against me this day. You Lord are my light and my salvation; whom shall I fear? You are my song and my strength; of whom shall I be afraid? This is my one true desire today and I will seek after it, that I may dwell in your presence, inquire in your temple, and behold your beauty all the day! I will trust you with all my heart and I will not

11

lean to my own understanding. I am assured that you will direct every step that I take today. From the rising of the sun until the going down of the same, your Name is a strong tower, and I am safe. You will perfect all that concerns me and bring all your purposes to pass and surely complete them.

Because your compassions fail not, I have new mercies every morning. My voice will you hear in the morning. I will direct my prayer to you and look up as I watch and wait for you to speak to my heart. Weeping and sorrow can endure only for a night, but joy comes in the morning. I say this is a good morning! Because of the power of your Word in my mouth, I am Energized, Inspired, Excited, Enthusiastic, Ecstatic and Expectant! In Jesus' Name... Amen!

Confessions

Psalm 5:3

"My voice shalt thou hear in the morning, O LORD; in the morning will I direct my prayer unto thee, and will look up."

Father this morning, I come into your presence with thanksgiving and with joy. This is the day that the Lord hath made, and I will rejoice and be glad in it. I enter your gates with thanksgiving and I come into your courts with praise. Father you have ordained praise because of your enemies. Out of my mouth I release praise that stills the enemy and the avenger. As I praise you, I draw strength from the well of salvation. All power and authority has been given to your Name, therefore; I exalt you. I lift up my voice to bless and extol you. You are great and greatly to be praised. You are the great King over all the earth. You are holy, you are great, and you are glorious — and I say HALLELUJAH! Your Name is a strong tower and the righteous run into it and they are safe. You are the God that

13

hears prayer. Your Word instructs me to pray and not faint lest Satan should get an advantage of me. I approach your throne of grace with my mouth filled with your Word.

I will pray fervently, accurately, and effectually, for this kind of prayer makes tremendous power available to me. You have promised when I pray according to your will, you hear me and I have those things that I desire when I pray. You have promised that what I ask for in your Name, I receive. Therefore, I ask that your Kingdom would come to the earth today and be revealed in every area of my life, my family, my ministry, my neighborhood, my city, and to the uttermost parts of the earth. I ask for only your will to be done. I decree that all your plans and desires will be fulfilled and carried out to the smallest detail — spiritually, personally, socially, and economically. I am blessed as I believe that there will be a performance of those things spoken to me by the Lord. I say that everything that pertains to life and godliness have been given to me. Therefore, I escape the corruption that is in this world, and I praise you as I become a partaker of your Divine nature. Today I say I am satisfied by the bread of heaven. For you Father give me my daily bread. You are my great Shepherd and I do not want or lack any good or beneficial thing. I bless you with all my soul for forgiving my iniquities and healing all my diseases.

Because I am forgiven, I make a righteous decision to forgive any and everyone. I thank you that my life is redeemed from destruction for you crowned me with love and compassion. You said I have what I say, so I open my mouth wide and say the Lord is my light and my salvation; whom shall I fear? The Lord is the strength of my life; of whom shall I be afraid?

My mouth is satisfied as I speak out the good things, and my youth is renewed like an eagle. Lead me away from temptation and every plan, plot, snare, trap, and scheme of my enemy. You O Lord order my steps in your Word, therefore; iniquity will not have dominion over me. You are my great deliverer! No evil shall befall me and no plague shall come near my dwelling. Because I have set my love upon you, you have promised to deliver me and set me on high. When I call upon you, you will answer me. You will be with me, honor me, satisfy me with long life, and continually show me your salvation. In Jesus' name, Amen.

I Will Confess Who I Am

I am Born of God.

I am a Son of God.

I am a Child of God.

I am led by the Spirit of God.

I am an heir of God and a joint heir with Christ.

I will joyfully confess my relationship with God.

I will take my place in the earth as a Son of God.

I don't live in this world by the will of flesh and blood or the merits of my own name, but I live by faith in the Son of God, who loved me and gave himself for me.

I am a Child of God!!!!

A Prayer of Repentance

Psalm 32:6

"Therefore, let everyone who is godly pray to You [for forgiveness] in a time when You [are near and] may be found; Surely when the great waters [of trial and distressing times] overflow they will not reach [the spirit in] him."

Father, I thank you and praise you for forgiveness of sin. I give blessings and glory to you for your great provision of the body of the Lord Jesus Christ and His precious blood that never loses its power. Thank you for your Holy Spirit that brings illumination and conviction to my heart and mind regarding the things that are contrary, defiant, and rebellious to your revealed will and desire for my life.

Your word says, "If we say we have no sin, we lie and contradict your Word and make you to be a liar," but if I confess my sin, you are faithful and just to forgive me and cleanse me from all unrighteousness."(1 John 1:8-10)

Father, I ask that you daily show me the sin that so easily besets me, the sin that I don't want to call sin, and the failure to come to you and receive the grace that is greater than all of my sins. Cause me to recognize the deception and pride that so cleverly covers my transgressions. Help me to accept that in me dwells no good thing; then lead me into the glorious light of repentance (the turning away from and forsaking the ways, ideals, feelings, thoughts, activities, and associations that hold me in the darkness of sin). Open my heart and my mind to the liberty that awaits me as I come humbly before you with a broken heart and contrite spirit. I am willing to receive the correction and chastisement that brings me into the righteousness that you have provided for me. You said, "In forsaking my ways, my thoughts and returning to you," you have promised you would have love, pity, and mercy on me and abundantly pardon my sins...

Enable me to feel the necessary pain that produces Godly sorrow (the pain you permit and direct that brings me to true repentance and leads to salvation and deliverance from evil). Give me an eagerness and earnestness to be clean and clear from all unrighteousness. Restore to me the joy of my salvation. Create in me a clean heart and renew a right, steadfast, persevering spirit within me. Thank you for being my hiding place and surrounding me with songs of deliverance. Instruct me and teach me in the way that I should go. Never cast me away from your presence, and don't take your Holy Spirit from me. (Psalm 51:11)

Loving Thy Law

Psalm 119:165

"Great peace have they who love thy law; nothing shall offend them or make them stumble."

Today I set my affections and my love on things that are above. Lord your Word is high above all, even your Name.

Thy Word is more pleasant to me than my daily bread. Because your law is in my heart, it causes me to delight in doing your will. Teach me the true love of your law, your ways, and your purpose in every area of life. To love you is to love your law and in loving your law, I am enabled to obey.

Father, you have warned me through your Word of the seduction and destruction that will come upon those who refuse to love thy law. Lord you alone know the lawlessness of my heart. Remove from me the way of falsehood and unfaithfulness to you and graciously impart your law to me. Open my eyes that I may behold wondrous things out of your law. I will not merely walk but run the way of your commandments when you give me a heart that is willing.

O Father, give me understanding that I might keep your law. I will observe it with my whole heart. Help me to daily understand and desire the life and truth that comes from hiding your law in my heart and the power of thy law to keep me from sinning against you. O Lord, I will love your law with all of my heart, soul, and strength! Amen!

Letting Go of the Past

Philippians 3:13

"Brothers and sisters, I do not consider that I have made it my own yet; but one thing I do: forgetting what lies behind and reaching forward to what lies ahead."

Today I close the door and all entrances and exits concerning my past.

Jesus, you said in Luke 9:62, "No one who puts his hand to the plow and looks back to the things behind him is fit for the Kingdom of God." I will not be disqualified from my Kingdom purpose or assignment by holding onto my past. I choose to forget the past and all that is behind me based on the power of your Word.

I make a Godly decision today to release all those who have hurt, rejected, deceived, and disappointed me. Father I ask you to forgive me for any role that I may have played in past activities, thoughts, words or deeds that did not please you. As I am forgiven, I am enabled to forgive others because only you are Righteous. From this day on, I will not rehearse or nurse the wounds or feelings associated with the past. The past is just what it is...the PAST. I will no longer be hindered or held back by the works or thoughts of the past. I have a bright new future and an eternal destiny! You Lord, have great plans for me, plans of peace and not evil and to give me a hope for my final outcome. I rise up now out of every place of oppression, pain, and failure that the past has held me in. I shake off the memory, and any remaining residue of defilement and abuse. Today I walk in the Truth, and the Truth sets me free spiritually, emotionally, mentally, and physically. Yes, He who the Son sets free is free indeed! Father, I pray for those who have hurt, violated and rejected me. I ask you to heal, deliver, and set them free also.

Your Word says, "You came to heal the broken-hearted" (Isaiah 61:1), so I bring the broken pieces of my heart and life to you...my Jehovah-Rapha...the Lord my Healer! You wipe all my tears away as you restore my soul. You give me joy in place of mourning and beauty for all the ashes pf my life. I can rejoice today because my life is hid with Christ in God! I am a new creature, old things have passed away and all things are made new. I say yes to your plans and purposes for me! I will not shrink back, step back, or fall back...I press forward toward the mark of the prize of the High calling of God in Christ Jesus. You said behold I do a new thing, therefore; I will fulfill your Kingdom assignment for my life as I walk today out of the past and into the light of a glorious future...I am free!!!

My Body; My Temple

1 Corinthians 6:19

"Do you not know that your body is a temple of the Holy Spirit who is within you, whom you have [received as a gift] from God, and that you are not your own [property]?"

O Lord, how awesome that you would choose to live in my body by your Holy Spirit. I give praise and thanksgiving to you for purchasing my body and redeeming it from destruction. Father, your desire in sending Jesus as my Redeemer is that you might live in me as at the beginning of my creation.

I proclaim this truth today, "my body is the Temple of the Living God, who has bought me with the precious blood of Jesus Christ, His only Son!" Because I am no longer my own, I have no more rights to this body, it belongs to you my God. I make a quality decision to honor you as I honor my body as your dwelling place. I call my body into submission through discipline. I buffet (treat roughly) and teach it to respond to the prompting and leading of my born-again Spirit. I refuse to let carnal appetites dictate to me through compulsive and addictive demands in any area. I take authority over my body members (eyes, ears, mouth, hands, and feet) that have been engaged in sinful, negative, and unproductive activities. I command them to now come into right alignment with my mind and heart, which are daily being renewed in the Word of God.

I refuse the vanity, lustful and corruptive desires of this world. I yield my body members to righteousness, as one who is alive from the dead. I say sin shall not have dominion over me. Every area of my body is set free and released to bring glory to God. I say the beauty of Holiness is in and upon my life and my body belongs to God. In Jesus' Name, Amen!

My Image

Genesis 1:26-27

"*Then God said, "Let Us (Father, Son, Holy Spirit) make man in Our image, according to Our likeness [not physical, but a spiritual personality and moral likeness]; and let them have complete authority over the fish of the sea, the birds of the air, the cattle, and over the entire earth, and over everything that creeps and crawls on the earth." So God created man in His own image, in the image and likeness of God He created him; male and female He created them. "*

I praise you Heavenly Father! You have created me in your very likeness and image. I was created for your highest pleasure. For you I was and am created. You formed my inward parts. You knit me together in my mother's womb. I was intricately and curiously wrought in secret. O how wonderful are your works. I have been born anew of your Spirit, not by the will of flesh and blood. I have been recreated in Christ Jesus. I am your handiwork! I walk in your pre-determined paths living the pre-arranged good life and doing the good works that you purposed for me beforehand.

Today, I claim and proclaim the Truths of your Word concerning who I am. I am complete in Jesus Christ my Lord. I have been raised up with Him to a new life. By the blood of Jesus Christ my Lord, I am forgiven. I have been made whole — spirit, soul, and body. I am set free and made to sit together with Christ in Heavenly places. I am healed and filled with the Holy Spirit of God.

I am delivered from the kingdom of darkness and translated into the Kingdom of God's dear Son. I have access into God's Holy Presence. I have the right to the Tree of Life. Nothing can separate me from the love of God. I can rejoice because I am a new creature. Old habits, ways, thoughts, and feelings have passed away. Your Spirit reminds me that I am a Son of God, whereby I can call you Abba Father. By your Word I cast down every false image and sabotaging thought about me. I have the Divine nature of God living in me. I walk in righteous paths and give glory to His Name.

My steps are ordered by the Lord. In exchange for all the ashes of my life, I clothe myself in beauty; I am glorious within. I am crowned with glory and honor. Joy and rejoicing are my portion. I have a rich inheritance; my identity is not marred or vague. When He appears, I shall be just like Him. As I behold you in your Word, I am changed into your image by your Holy Spirit. I reign as King in life through Jesus Christ. As you are, so am I. Thank you Father for a New Image!!!

Learning to Wait

Psalm 62:5

"My soul, wait thou only upon God; for my expectation is from him."

Father, you have promised that in waiting on you, I am renewed. You alone know the restlessness of my soul, the wandering of my mind, the ups and downs of my emotions, and the dominance of my will. Yet you have promised that there is victory in learning to wait and being still before you. Lord, you call my soul to rest and wait patiently for you. O deliver me from the anxiousness of my soul, and teach me the power and confidence of waiting on you. Holy Spirit help me not to fret. Teach me to cease from anger and let go of every injustice.

Bring me into the grace of being anxious for nothing. Today, I commit my way and the path I take unto you, my Lord. I will trust and delight myself in you. Thank you that my steps have already been ordered, and you Lord delight in the way I take. Your instruction to wait does not exempt me from the righteous activity of "doing good (Ps.34:14)," eparting from evil, being meek, seeking peace, and committing my ways to you. Father, as I obey your commands, I begin to mount up over every obstacle and hindrance to my spiritual progress. I run and do not feel weary. I walk without fainting. This is the blessing of waiting on the Lord. Wait for, hope in, and expect the Lord. Wait I say upon the Lord. (Psalm 27)

Trust in the Lord

Isaiah 26:3-4

"You will keep in perfect and constant peace the one whose mind is steadfast [that is, committed and focused on You—in both inclination and character], Because he trusts and takes refuge in You [with hope and confident expectation]. "Trust [confidently] in the LORD forever [He is your fortress, your shield, your banner], For the LORD GOD is an everlasting Rock [the Rock of Ages]."

O Lord, thou have promised to keep me in perfect peace and to sustain me as I keep my mind stayed on you because I trust in you!

You Lord instruct me through your Word to trust in you forever, for in the Lord Jehovah is everlasting strength. My trust in you expresses my unmovable and unshakable confidence in you. I will not lean to my own understanding, but in all my ways I will acknowledge you and you will give direction to all my paths. In an age where men trust in the chariots and horses of worldly strength and power, I choose to trust and fully rely upon the Name, Power, Authority, and Goodness of the Lord.

Unto thee, O Lord, do I lift up my soul. O my God I put my trust in you, for you will not allow me to be put to shame. Neither shall my enemies triumph over me. (Psalm 25:1-2)

Daily I will wait upon you in childlike faith and trust you though I stand in utter despair. I declare that even if you slay me, I will trust you. For you know the way that I take. All your plans and paths for me are good!

Father I thank and praise you for guiding my soul into this place of quiet rest. I can wait on you and be of good courage because I am trusting in you. I am leaning fully upon you and you will never fail me. O my soul trust ye in the Lord Forever!

My Peace

John 14:27

"Peace I leave with you; My [perfect] peace I give to you; not as the world gives do I give to you. Do not let your heart be troubled, nor let it be afraid. [Let My perfect peace calm you in every circumstance and give you courage and strength for every challenge.]"

I give praise and thanksgiving to you, Jesus. You have given and bequeathed to me your very own peace. Because of this rich and beneficial gift, I will not allow my heart to be troubled or afraid.

I will stop allowing myself to be agitated, disturbed, intimidated, or unsettled. Yes I say that it is well with my soul because your peace like a river, attends my way! Every thought of discouragement, fear, and anxiety have to bow down and shrink away in the presence of your peace.

As the Captain of my soul, you speak peace to the winds and waves that rise up in overwhelming and boisterous confrontation within and around me. Father, the capstones of your Kingdom are Righteousness, Peace, and Joy, in the Holy Spirit. When I walk in peace, I walk in the realm of the Kingdom of Heaven. In that place, I have peace that surpasses all earthly understanding. I am anxious for nothing! As I communicate with God my Father in prayer, supplication, and thanksgiving, I make my request known.

Your unfailing peace mounts up over my heart and my mind as a Divine guard, keeping, defending, and protecting my deepest emotions and thoughts. In that tranquil state of quietness and confidence, I experience peace like an umpire settling with finality every resistant and opposing force arrayed against me. Jesus, your peace keeps me as I purpose to keep my mind fixed and focused on you. I trust you with every decision and concern of my life, for in you the Lord Jehovah, is everlasting strength.

Father, your Priestly blessing upon my life gives me peace. You watch over me by lifting up your approving countenance upon me and making your face to shine upon me as you give mercy, grace, and favor.

Thank you for being the Prince of my Peace. Daily I am being conformed to your will and finding great peace. I am learning to love your laws, your precepts, and your commands. Nothing is able to offend me or make me stumble. In every relationship I will pursue peace, even if I have to run after it. Because I am a son of God, I am a peace maker.

When ill will, strife, and confusion arise, I will speak words of comfort and truth. I will sow seeds of peace as I work to make peace, first in myself and then in others; the peace that brings harmony and agreement to every situation.

Your wisdom in me is first of all pure and undefiled. It is peace-loving, courteous, considerate, and gentle. This is not the false peace that the world gives. Jesus, you are my Jehovah Shalom! You have made peace with God for me by your sacrificial and obedient death on the cross.

I have been brought near to God my Father, by the power of the Holy Spirit and have bold confident access into His presence by your blood. Father, you have spoken peace to your people, those who are in right standing with you. Mercy and Truth have met together, and Righteousness and Peace have kissed each other.

I speak peace today over my life, my marriage, my family, my ministry, and all those who serve the Lord with me. Over my community and city and every path you have given me to walk in. Peace to the nations and peace to your Holy City Jerusalem. May peace be within your walls!

I thank you Father God for wrapping me in peace and surrounding me like the walls surrounded Jerusalem. Amen!

Distractions

Luke 10:38-42

"Now it came to pass, as they went, that he entered into a certain village: and a certain woman named Martha received him into her house. And she had a sister called Mary, which also sat at Jesus' feet, and heard his word. But Martha was cumbered about much serving, and came to him, and said, Lord, dost thou not care that my sister hath left me to serve alone? Bid her therefore that she help me. And Jesus answered and said unto her, Martha, Martha, thou art careful and troubled about many things: But one thing is needful: and Mary hath chosen that good part, which shall not be taken away from her."

In this passage of scripture He taught to be distracted is to be overly occupied and too busy for spending time with the Lord and receiving His Word. He also revealed that it creates anxiousness and troubling about many things. Daily we choose the better portion, which cannot be taken from me, which is to our advantage and cannot be taken from us.

Today I make a decision to refuse distractions in any and all forms. I will not be scattered in my thinking or doing. I will recognize all subtle seductions made through infirmity, pleasure, discouragement, enticement, and even what appears to be beneficial. I agree with the Word of God that says, "All things are lawful unto me, but all things are not expedient (helpful). All things are lawful for me, and I will not be brought under the power of any." (I Corinthians 6:12 KJV)

I thank you Jesus for the Holy Spirit that you have given to me, who leads and guides me into all Truth! Holy Spirit, you have given me the gift of discernment, whereby I am well able to determine what is of God.

When the enemy comes in like a flood, your Spirit raises up a standard against him. Today, I rise up in the power of the Holy Spirit and I resist and defeat all satanic assignments sent against me. I will do all that I have been given to do and accomplish every task assigned to me by the sufficiency of God's grace. As I dwell in the secret place of the Most High, I refocus my energies and regroup my thoughts. No evil can befall me, nor can any plague come nigh my dwelling place. I will not be drawn out of God's presence or my place of obedience.

Thank you Father for the angelic assignment concerning me, that keeps me in all of my ways. And though a thousand may fall at my side and ten thousand at my right hand, they shall not come nigh me. Hallelujah! I say, "I am covered with your feathers and under the safety of your wings I will trust." I will run this race with joy as I turn from all distractions and fix my eyes on you. Distractions be gone in the name of Jesus!!!! Holy Spirit you are my truth-guide, gift-giver, standard-raiser, yoke-destroyer, chain-breaker, word-teacher, and secret-revealer. As I submit to you, the devil is fleeing.

Breakthrough Prayer

Psalm 18:40

"Thou hast also given me the necks of mine enemies; that I might destroy them that hate me."

The weapons of my warfare are not carnal but MIGHTY through God. In the name of the resurrected Lord, Jesus Christ, I come against the spirit of: INTERFERENCE, INTERRUPTION, and INTERCEPTION of all necessary communications, provisions, assistance, and all people who are assigned to my good and my ministry calling. You Lord give me the necks of my enemies. I decree and declare that, at the voice of the Lord, all resistant forces and allegiances FALL and FAIL before me. I WAR for the release of all rightful resources and unexpected blessings NOW! I call forth a divine release and a swift delivery of ALL rightful possessions TODAY in Jesus name!!!

No-Thing is Impossible

Luke 1:37

"For with God nothing [is or ever] shall be impossible."

You are the Great God Elohim is your Name. Adonai Lord and Master, I give your Name the Praise. O Lord my God, thou hast made the heavens and the earth by thy great power and outstretched arm. There is no-thing too hard for Thee.

You have said, "Behold I am the Lord the God of all flesh, is there anything too hard for Me?" Father I bless you and thank you for your Word. In the face of every difficult and impossible situation, I am reminded that no-thing is impossible with you! Today my mouth is enlarged over my enemies. I make my declaration of faith: "With God nothing is impossible, and there is no Word from you that is without power to be fulfilled."

Lord I praise and bless you, for you are not a man that you should lie. You have said it, therefore, you shall do it, and because you have said it, I can say it. I speak to every mountain in my life, every difficult task and every impossible thing and say "Be Thou Removed." I face lack, inability, disappointment, and failure with faith in God. For the things that are impossible with man are possible with God. (Luke 18:27)

I say today, "Be it done unto me according to your Word, for no Word from God is without power to be performed." (Luke 1:47, 48) I bless the Lord with all my soul. My spirit rejoices in God, my Savior, for He has regarded my low estate."

I am blessed because I believe that there will be a performance of all that has been spoken to me from the Lord. Father, I praise and thank you that your Word does not fail neither does it return to you void. You watch over your Word to perform it. Your Word God will accomplish all that it is sent to do. Therefore, I will bless the Lord with all my soul and praise and exalt you for your mighty angels who do your commands. They hearken to the voice of your Word. Thank you Lord. As I confess your Word, I give voice to your will and the angels carry it out. For every situation that I have limited you, I take the limits off by your Word. No-thing is impossible. I will not stagger in unbelief or distrust, nor will I waiver in doubt or question you concerning your Word.

I will grow strong and be empowered by faith in my God. I continually give praise and glory to you, for you are able and mighty to keep your Word and do what you have promised. So I say, "Be it done unto me according to your Word."

No-Thing Is Impossible!!

It is Written

Luke 4:4

"And Jesus answered him, saying, It is written, That man shall not live by bread alone, but by every word of God."

Today I take the Word of God in my mouth as the Mighty Sword of the Spirit. Jesus, you are the High Priest of my confession. You are my great example for Victory. Therefore, I will have what I say because what I say has been said by the mouth of God. Not only has God said it, but it is written! I defeat and destroy every work of Satan by the words of my mouth. I choose life that I and my seed might live. I will enjoy life as the fruit of my tongue. Today, I am far from the thoughts of oppression and destruction. I will not fear or be in terror for none of these things shall come near me.

I shall establish myself in righteousness, in conformity with God's will and God's order. I will never be ashamed or confounded, nor will I be depressed. You Lord are my Maker, my Husband. The Lord of Hosts is your Name.

Your loving kindness shall never depart from me, nor shall your Covenant of peace and completeness be removed. Behold, they may gather together and stir up strife, but whoever stirs up strife against me shall fall and surrender to me. No weapon, no plan of hurt, defeat, or destruction shall prosper against me. In Christ Jesus I have peace, righteousness, and security and I will triumph over any and all opposition. This is my heritage as a servant of the Lord. Father, I praise you today that all my needs are richly met in Christ Jesus my Lord.

For every sickness — I have health.

In trouble — I have peace that passes my understanding.

When I am weak — Your strength is made perfect in me.

When I lack — You reveal yourself as Jehovah Jireh, my provider.

When I can't see my way — Your Word is a lamp to my feet and a light to my path.

When I am cast down — You Lord are my glory and the lifter up of my head.

When my heart is overwhelmed — You lead me to the Rock that is higher than I.

When the enemy comes in like a flood — Your Spirit raises up a standard against him. You teach my hands to war and my fingers to fight my arms break a bow of steel. By thee, I run through troops and leap over walls. I tread upon serpents and scorpions and over all the power of the enemy — Nothing shall harm me, for you, Father, have given your angels charge over me.

I eat the good of the land.

I am blessed coming in and going out. My home is blessed; my storehouse and my bank accounts are blessed. My family is blessed, saved, and delivered.

The Holy Spirit of Truth teaches me and guides me in all my paths. I walk in the wisdom of God. I have divine intelligence regarding everything that pertains to life and godliness. I have the mind of Christ.
I walk worthy of this calling and I am fruitful in every good work.

The works of my hands are blessed. My feet possess the land as I fulfill my kingdom assignment in the earth.

You Lord will make known to all that you are with me.

I give praise and glory to you God, for you are great and greatly to be praised.

My lips shall praise thee. Thus will I bless thee.

I hold fast to this confession of faith, for it has a great reward.

In Jesus' Name, Amen!

Family Prayer

Ephesians 3:15

"Every family in heaven and earth is named. From you all fatherhood takes its title and derives its name."

Family is your heart and desire. John 10:10 says, "The thief comes to steal, kill, and destroy, but I (Jesus) have come that you might have life and have it more abundantly." From the beginning of time the thief has plagued family relationships. But for this purpose the Son of God was manifest to undo, destroy, loosen, and dissolve the works that the devil has done. All things come into existence by the Word of God, who speaks of the non-existent things that He promised as if they already existed. Therefore, I say my family is saved, blessed, healed, restored, and victorious! When human reason for hope is gone, I refuse to weaken or stagger in my faith. No unbelief or distrust will make me waiver, doubtingly question, or stagger at the promises of God. I will grow strong in my faith, as I am assured that my God is able to keep His Word and do what He has promised.

Father, I lay the axe of your Word to the root of the family destroying spirit assigned to my family. I go back into the bloodline of 10 generations and apply the blood of Jesus Christ of Nazareth to every generational sin and curse. I decree a new bloodline of victory. According to Exodus 17:14, you Lord have sworn to war and destroy the Amalekite spirit from under the heavens. This is the spirit that disregards, resists, and fights against the spiritual inheritance of families.

My family will release one another from all debts of hurt, anger, arrogance, rebellion, dishonor, pride, un-forgiveness, alienation, abandonment, rejection, disapproval, disappointment, jealousy, rivalry, perfection, performance, and any known or unknown sins that have been committed. Father, I ask that you forgive us ALL. I sever all roots of bitterness so the next generation will not be defiled. I renounce dysfunctional relationships, and receive the ability to function as a God-designed family. Because our hearts are full of the love of God, we have love, one for another and are always ready to pardon and overlook a wrong done. I choose to believe, hope, and endure all things because this love can never fail.

I decree a new beginning for my family as we experience the blessing of dwelling together in unity. I say the former tyrant masters are dead, and they shall not live and reappear. I say they are powerless ghosts. They shall not rise and come back. You Lord have made an end to them and have caused every memory and every trace of their supremacy to perish. (Isaiah 26:14 AMP) I give thanks and praise to you my Father, for you have given us the victory! I will continually acknowledge and bless your name! In view of your great and precious promises, I will give all diligence to add to my faith; virtue, goodness of character, knowledge, temperance, patience, godliness, brotherly kindness and love. For if these things are in us, we shall never be barren or unfruitful, and we will never fall or fail (2 Peter 1:5-10). Jesus, you are the Sovereign Lord of my family!

A Prayer for Youth

Ecclesiastes 12:1

"Remember now thy Creator in the days of thy youth, while the evil days come not, nor the years draw nigh, when thou shalt say, I have no pleasure in them."

Father, I thank and praise you that I can come to you in my youth. Your Word instructs me to remember you my creator, in the days of my youth. I ask you to forgive me for the foolish mindsets and activities of my youthfulness and cause me to understand that the decisions I make in my youth are the most important decisions of my life. Your warnings are beneficial to me so that I don't waste the strength and vitality of my youth on the vanities of this life. In your great wisdom, you challenge me to live for you early so that I don't experience the painful regrets of disobedience to my God in old age.

Father, there is no excuse for my ignorance or lack of knowledge in living for you. Psalm 119:9-11 tells me I can cleanse my ways by heeding to your Word, and that by hiding your Word in my heart, I can turn from sin. Holy Spirit, deliver me from the deadly desires of this age that thrive on instant gratification through food, money, sex, entertainment, and selfish achievements. Cause me to recognize the long-term consequences of worldly lusts. Empower me to flee from youthful lusts and desires that I might run the race that you have set before me and win! Cause me to regard with great respect the parents, spiritual leaders, and mentors you have placed in my life. Remind me that instruction saves me from destruction. A fool despises instruction, but a wise man heeds instruction and correction. *Many of the Proverbs were originally addressed to young men because they were expected to inherit the leadership of their families and nation.*

Father, your intent in making me a Son of God is so that I would inherit the rich blessings and the honor of leadership in your Kingdom. You have made me to be a King and Priest unto you. As I embrace the true fear of the Lord, I will walk in wisdom, insight, and understanding concerning every path of life. I rejoice in my youth as I make a quality decision to love the Lord my God with all my heart, mind, soul and strength. This is the conclusion and full purpose of life; fear God and keep His commandments!

In Honor of Mothers

Ephesians 6:2

"Honor thy father and mother; which is the first commandment with promise."

Father, I thank you for the privilege of honoring my mother. I understand that my origin and substance is from you, yet you chose to use the womb of a woman to nurture me until the day of my birth. I want to say "thank you" to my Mother who said yes to your will concerning me.

I thank you that I was not aborted, miscarried, stillborn, or discarded. Lord I recognize that in her humanness, she perhaps didn't do everything right, or to my expectations. Yet I choose to forgive and release her from any debt of failure.

I bless and thank you. For without my Mother, I would not be on planet Earth today. Your Word teaches me to honor my Father and Mother (without condition or exception) that my life may be long upon the Earth. This is the first commandment with a promise. I know and believe that you are a promise keeper, therefore, I will do what you command and give honor to my Mother.

For the Mothers who have gone to their resting place, we will give thanks always at every remembrance of them and for those who yet live. We thank you for their life. Help me to honor all Mothers as unto you. We pray blessings of strength and peace upon their lives. We ask that the joy of the Lord be their daily portion.

Father, I ask that all the things that I and others have done to bring our mothers sorrow would now be turned into joy and dancing! As their seed, we will rise up and call them blessed!

Help us not to violate your law concerning my Mother by failing to care and provide for her even unto her old age. Teach us to do and say the things that make her proud to be our Mother. We make a decision give honor to her all the days of our lives. In Jesus' Name, Amen.

Praying for the City

Jeremiah 29:7

"And seek the peace of the city whither I have caused you to be carried away captives, and pray unto the LORD for it: for in the peace thereof shall ye have peace."

The weapons of our warfare are not carnal, but they are mighty through God. I establish a fiery hedge of Holy Ghost protection in, and around the city of _____, our homes, our ministries, our businesses, and our neighborhoods. I raise up the mighty bulwark of the Holy Spirit and call for myriads of angels to establish divine command posts at all four corners of the city of _____. I decree that Holy Spirit-filled intercessors will awake out of their sleep and return to their assigned positions of prayer. They will stand upon their watches around the walls of the city and give You, God, no rest until the city becomes a praise.

Father, I take this assignment in the faith of Joshua, who obeyed your command and led a people into spiritual warfare and saw a tremendous victory at the shout of their praise! I say every wall of separation, every satanic stronghold and every resistance to my prayers will fall at the sound of my praise. Lord, I say the city of_____ will not miss its season of visitation. As I get up on my post, I will see what you will say (Habakkuk 2:1). I will stand immovable in my God-ordained position in spite of how it looks, because I walk by faith and not by sight. Father, I ask you to establish warring angel's at all four gates of this city and to release your fiery sword against all satanic works that seek to gain entrance.

I speak now to murderous spirits that have been assigned to the city of _____. I say your weapons will not prosper. I speak failure and destruction to all of your works, for the Lord of Hosts has given me power to tread upon all the works of Satan. You Lord, give us the necks of our enemies that we might destroy all who hate us. We war for the release of demonically held neighborhoods in our city and all areas that are satanically saturated with the works of evil. We take our communities for the Kingdom of God. By the authority given to me by your Name, your Blood, and your Word. We bind, chain, curse, and cause to fail every scheme, plot, database, and command center of the kingdom of darkness. We send confusion into the enemies' camp. You Lord, cause them to turn on one another and bring destruction to all their works. We call every captive son, daughter, husband, father, mother, sister, and brother to be released by the Word of God and return to their land (Jeremiah 31:17).

Because of the anointing, I decree yokes broken, chains destroyed, blinded eyes to see, deaf ears to hear, lame and feeble legs to not only walk, but run. We speak to the gates of hell and say, "You shall not prevail against us." We call our heritage back to their land and their place of blessings and productivity. We raise up a mighty shield of faith around this city and say our city is a city of Truth and the city of a great King and Jesus Christ is Lord!

WE SHOUT NOW!!!!

Kingdom Declaration

Luke 11:2

"He said to them, "When you pray, say: 'Father, hallowed be Your name. Your kingdom come."

The Kingdom of God/Heaven is a Spiritual Kingdom, having no origin in this world. It extends beyond the limitations of the material world in which we live and is not limited to what is visible or tangible. The Kingdom cannot be recognized or embraced except by the Holy Spirit of God, who is the great Executive Administrator of the Kingdom. He alone is the Divine Workman who executes and carries out fully the mind of God according to John 16:13-15. *But when He, the Spirit of Truth (the Truth-giving Spirit) comes, He will guide you into all the Truth, the whole, full Truth.*

For He will not speak His own message (on His own authority), but He will tell whatever He hears from the Father. He will give the message that has been given to Him, and He will announce and declare to you the things that are to come (that will happen in the future). He will honor and glorify me, because He will take of (receive, draw upon) what is mine and will reveal (declare, disclose, transmit) to you. Everything the Father has is mine. That is what I meant when I said, "He, the Spirit, will take the things that are mine and will reveal it to you." Jesus, our High Priest is in the Heavens as the Head of the Church. He has sent the Holy Spirit into the Earth/world as the revealer of all things pertaining to the Kingdom (Ephesians 1:19-23), so that you can know and understand that which is the immeasurable and unlimited and surpassing greatness of His power in and for us who believe, as demonstrated in the working of His mighty strength, which He exerted in Christ when He raised Him up from the dead and seated Him at His own right hand in the heavenly places.

He is far above all rule and authority and power and dominion and every name that is named above. Every title that can be conferred, not only in this age and in this world, but also in the age and the world which is to come. He has put all things under His feet and has appointed Him the universal and supreme Head of the Church (a headship exercised throughout the Church, which is His Body, the fullness of Him Who fills all in all). Apart from the Holy Spirit, we continue to walk as citizens of the kingdoms of this world. Filled and controlled by the Holy Spirit of God, we rise above every power, influence, and limitation of this world. Though we are in this world, we are not of this world (do not have our origin or citizenship here).

We Say:

Our words are spiritual and full of power
Our laws, rules, and ways are spiritual
Our bread and water are spiritual
Our medicine is spiritual
Our weapons of warfare are spiritual
Our prayer and praise are spiritual
Our eyesight is spiritual
Our hearing is spiritual
Our wisdom and knowledge are spiritual
Our influence steers the unseen realm and brings the
Kingdom of Heaven into what is seen
Our resources, money, time, and talents have spiritual
purpose and rewards
We have life even though we pass through death
We are from another Kingdom
And our King has conquered the world!!!

Thy Kingdom Come!!!

Victory

1 Corinthians 15:57

"But thanks be to God, which giveth us the victory through our Lord Jesus Christ."

Thanks be unto You oh Lord, for You have given me the victory. And this is the victory that overcometh the world, even my faith. Jesus, today I place my life, my family, my ministry, my needs, my desires, my hopes, my future and every concern of my heart into Your hands. My faith stands and rest in Your words, "Fear not, for I have overcome the world."

Thank You for every trial and every test of my faith. For all that You have permitted, and yet lovingly observed that I will not be destroyed. Thank You for causing me to see the dark places and the unsubmitted places in my heart, and enabling me to recognize the weakness of my faith, and my lack of trust in You.

Thank You Father that the enemy was exposed in his plots and schemes, and was not able or allowed to triumph over me. For this I give Your name great praise! As I praise and bless Your excellent name, the enemy is stealed and made to be silent. You have ordained and established praise forever. Therefore I rise up and I go forth out of every place of fear and inadequacy, lack, doubt and oppression. For You have called and caused me to come up hither, and to sit with You in heavenly places; far above all principalities, powers and rulers of darkness.

Your glory adorns me and lifts up my head. Your Light shines and makes me radiant, and lovely all together. Your shield defends me and Your Word—the Sword of the Spirit—defeats every work of the evil one.

Today I walk in truth concerning Your great salvation. I am the head and not the tail. I am above and never beneath. I am blessed from the time I rise up until the time I lay down; and even while I sleep, You are giving to me. I lay down in peace and I awake in righteousness. Wisdom crowns my day and gives direction to my path. As I worship and wait at Your gate. You open to me Your rich treasury in the heavens, and You bless me with every spiritual blessing that I have need of. You favor me and You cause men to do likewise. You are working great good for me out of every pain and shame of my past. You will make known to all Your great faithfulness to me. Lord, I will trust You and wait expectedly for all that You have promised to do. My heart rejoices in God—my great King—Who rules and reigns over everything. My faith has increased as my flesh has decreased.

Because I am justified and sanctified by the finished work by Jesus Christ my Lord, I walk by faith and not by sight. Faith in You my Lord and all that You have spoken and decreed concerning me. Your words gives sight to my spiritual eyes and causes me to call things that be not as though they were. I will contend for the faith in every arena I am called to stand in; and having done all to stand, I will stand therefore. For without faith I can never please You, my Lord.

As I pray, I will pray in faith; believing all things that I ask and that are in agreement with You, You will give to me. I have strong confidence that whatever I ask, I receive.

Thanks be unto You oh Lord my God, for the victory! Like the dawning of a new day. For every place of wrestling and watching in my life, You have given me victory!

Song unto the Lord: Thank You Lord for victory. Thank You Lord, You opened my eyes to see; I say, thank You Lord for the victory. Thank You Lord. I say thank You...thank You Lord...

Church Arise

Romans 1:16-17

For I am notashamed of the gospel of Christ: for it is the power of God unto salvation to every one that believeth; to the Jew first, and also to the Greek.For therein isthe righteousness of God revealed from faith to faith: as it is written, The just shall live by faith.

Lord, we are not ashamed of the Gospel of Jesus Christ; for it is the power of Salvation to everyone that believeth. Lord, we ask today that Your Gospel would come reform; refine, and revive Your Church. May the Church no longer deny the power thereof. Pull down the form of godliness and purify to yourself a peculiar people. Make us to be those that will wait and hope in your great redemption of mankind.

Bring down the enemies of Your Church—Your Holy Body. The spiritual forces that have arrayed itself. God, destroy them according to Your Word in 1 John 3:8—You said "for this purpose was the Son of God manifest". Bring desolation and utter destruction to all oppressing spirits. For you said in Isaiah 54, we "shall be far from oppression"; and that no weapon that is formed against Your Church shall prosper.

As in the days of old, send out Your arrows! Release your fury against the powers of this age. Rise up, oh God! Display your power to conquer and spoil the powers of darkness. Bring down every earthly power, authority, system and kingdom that has set itself against the Lord, and His anointed. Break them, oh God, with your rod of iron. Spoil principalities and powers, and openly show them to be nothing, as you triumph over them!

Establish Your Kingdom in our hearts, and within our land and our City. You are the Great Redeemer of all men. Enable us to endure and remain faithful as we see the distress and tribulation of this age. Deliver us from siding with and minding earthly things that lead to destruction and doom. Keep us from the devouring fire of your jealousy. Restore and revive our peace and our prosperity. Make way for the accomplishment of your purpose within us.

Take away our sin and cure us from our idolatries and the corruptions of our heart. Give us pure speech that we may no longer speak profaneness and falsehood. Cause our speech be seasoned with grace. May our worship of you, our God, be according to Your will. May our prayer be the spiritual offering with which you are most honored. Let the words of our mouth and the meditations of our heart be acceptable in Thy sight. Make us unanimous in our service, that we may be one, as our Lord Jesus prayed.

Grant us the priestly blessing of unity as we offer ourselves to you as living sacrifices. Lord, we will draw nigh to you with the acceptable sacrifice of praise, prayer and almsgiving. Jesus, Your High Priest prayer was for us to be sanctified by Your Word of Truth. Father, release Your converting power to save and convert sinners to the knowledge of Truth. Remove the profane from your house—Your Holy Place. Expose the hypocrite—the pretenders of holiness, and all that is offensive to You. Raise up your remnant of holy, humble, service minded people, whose devotion is wholeheartedly for you. And though we may be greatly afflicted in this world, let our trust in you reveal the greatness of your majesty, and your power, and your glory.

We will rejoice in the abundance of your purity and Your peace. Your richness shall be our pure delight. We will know no fear; for no one shall make us afraid. For where iniquity is erased, calamity has no place. Instead of hopelessness and despair; we lift our hands and our hearts in prayer, as the joy of the Lord strengths us.

We say our King—the King of Glory—is in our midst! Therefore, we lift up our heads as the gates of the Lord; and we will be lifted up as your everlasting doors! And we declare the King of Glory shall come in; the Lord strong and mighty! For you Lord shall be admired and glorified in the midst of your Church.

And we say "AMEN SO BE IT!" Let the Church rise…

Alice J. Jones

Available Products

CD's
My House "A House of Prayer & Praise"
My Heart "A Heart of Worship"
The Power of Early Morning Prayer
All Manner of Prayer
We Set the Atmosphere

Teachings
Principle, Power & Purpose of Praise
The Church, The Church, The Church
Arise, Shine & Be Radiant

Books
The Storehouse – God's Plan for the Tithe
All Manner of Prayer
Daily Steps in Truth and more…

Messages
Pure and Undefiled Religion
The Fame & Glory of Prayer
Stay in the Number
A Righteous Realm
The Power & Reality of Our Identity

More Messages
The Gospel
The Lord Shall Reign in the Midst of Zion
Oh the Blood
Components of Spiritual Victory

Contact Information
Alice J. Jones
2131 E. 54th Street
Indianapolis, IN 46220
www.AliceJJones.org
317-252-2710

Social Media
Twitter - AJJMinistries

Instagram - AJJMinistries

Facebook - Alice J. Jones Ministries

Made in the USA
Charleston, SC
28 February 2016